This book is dedicated
To my grandchildren, who will continue to enjoy the Northwest Arm.
— Heather Watts

Formac Publishing Company Limited acknowledges the support of the cultural affairs section, Nova Scotia Department of Tourism and Culture. We acknowledge the financial support of the Government of Canada through the Book Publishing Industry Development Program (BPIDP) for our publishing activities.

We acknowledge the support of the Canada Council for the Arts for our publishing program.

National Library of Canada Cataloguing in Publication

Watts, Heather, 1936-
Halifax's Northwest Arm : an illustrated history / by Heather Watts and Michele Raymond; preface by Janet Kitz.

ISBN 0-88780-606-6

    1. Northwest Arm Bay (Halifax, N.S.)—History—Pictorial works.
I. Raymond, Michele II. Title.
FC2346.56.R38 2003   971.6'225   C2003-903904-8

Formac Publishing Company Limited
5502 Atlantic Street,
Halifax, Nova Scotia B3H 1G4
www.formac.ca

Printed and bound in the People's Republic of China

To my father, Richard L. Raymond, who first brought me to the shores of the Northwest Arm.
— Michèle Raymond

Visual Sources and Credits:

AGNS – Art Gallery of Nova Scotia; MSHS – Mainland South Heritage Society; NSM – History Collection, Nova Scotia Museum

Cover, AGNS; page 5, Photo Keith Vaughan; page 7, private collection ; page 8 AGNS ; page 9 Randall House Museum, Wolfville; page 10 AGNS; page 11 (above) AGNS; page 11, below, page 12, NSM; page 12, below, Henry Mayhew and John Binney, *The Criminal Prison of London and Scenes of Prison Life* (Frank Cass & Co. Ltd., London, 1968); page 13, private collection; page 14, above, "Halifax the Garrison City" (MacFarlane, Toronto n.d.); below, NSM; page 15, Photo Gary Castle; page 16 AGNS,; page 17, "Halifax, N.S. and Vicinity" (Valentine and Sons, n.d.); page 18 AGNS; page 19, NSM; page 20, below AGNS, Canadian Illustrated News; page 21 AGNS; page 22, *Oxford History of the Prison* (New York,1995); page 23 NSARM; page 24, left, NSARM; right, above and below, Mayhew and Binny, ibid.; page 26, National Archives of Canada C-116867; page 27, above, NSARM Portrait 5785 by Robert Field, below, NSARM; page 28, Dalhousie Art Gallery; page 29 NSM; page 30, top P.B. Waite, Lives of Dalhousie University Vol 1 (McGill-Queens, 1994); middle, NSARM; bottom, L.J. and Joan Payzant, Like a Weaver's Shuttle (Nimbus, 1980); page 32 top and below, NSARM; page 33 above NSM, below, Photo Gary Castle; pages 34, 35, 36, NSARM; page 37, Janina Konczacki (ed.) *Victorian Explorer* (Nimbus 1994; page 38. NSARM; page 39, 40, below, 41, 42, 43, all, 46, 47, NSARM; page 48, private collection; page 49, NSARM; page 51, *Victorian Lady's Album* (Formac); page 51, CP Archives; page 52, below left, private collection ; right, upper, NSARM; page 53, private collection; page 54, MSHS / Harvie; page 56, MSHS; page 57, top left and middle, St. John the Baptist Church, top right, MSHS; bottom, left, private collection; bottom right, Bethany Church; ; pages 58 and 59 all private collections; page 60, NSARM; page 62 above, NSM; page 64, NSARM; page 64 above, NSARM, below, "Halifax, N.S. and Vicinity" (Valentine and Sons, n.d.); page 66, below left, MSHS; page 67, AGNS; page 68, top, MSHS / Gilkie; below, left, NSM; page 70, top, Waegwoltic Club; page 71, Saraguay Club.

TABLE OF CONTENTS

ACKNOWLEDGEMENTS

Literally hundreds of people have helped us in this project, passing on anecdote or fact, or news of one more sketch of the Northwest Arm hidden away somewhere. We owe particular thanks, however, to a few among them: Wilma Ackerlund, Ray and Bernice Bignell, the late Theda (Forward) Brodie, Janet Chute, Greg Cochkanoff, Brian Cuthbertson, Ruth Draper, Gordon Fader, Phyllis Fenerty, Hilda Gilkie and the late Roy Gilkie, Margaret Grant, Margaret Haliburton, Hugh and Sheila Kindred, Janet Kitz, Kay Finley Mack, Bill Martin, Guy MacLean, Dr. Alan Marble, Vivien Morrison, Mora Dianne O'Neill, Walter Piers, Anita Price, Dorothy Read, Warren Robertson, Alan Ruffman, Peter Saulnier, Lucy Scott-Bonise, Mike Slayter, Marjorie Swingler, Alison Watts.

We thank the staff of the following institutions: Nova Scotia Archives and Records Management (especially Philip Hartling, John MacLeod, Garry Shutlak and Lois Yorke), Dalhousie Special Collections (Karen E. Smith), Maritime Command Museum (Marilyn Gurney), Nova Scotia Museum (especially Scott Robson, Alex Wilson and Ruth Whitehead), and the Art Gallery of Nova Scotia (Judy Dietz).

We acknowledge J.W. Regan, whose *Sketches and Traditions of the Northwest Arm* (1908) launched us on our way and Richard Rivers' MSc thesis, "The Rise and Fall of Amateur Rowing on the Northwest Arm" (1975).

Above all, we thank Iris Shea whose knowledge of the western shore of the Arm is unparalleled, and who has been unfailingly generous in sharing it. And we are grateful to Derek Watts and Jocelyn Raymond Read who have each been tireless in lending patient support and a perceptive eye to this project.

FOREWORD

On a map, the Northwest Arm appears as a narrow channel that, rather inconveniently, splits mainland Halifax. It would be hard to envisage a more picturesque barrier. On a dark winter's night, more than thirty years ago, I first came to live in Canada, to a house on the shore of the Arm. My pleasure and enchantment at the view has never diminished. Binoculars lie conveniently to hand at four different windows. Meals are eaten by a window, and the computer is backed by that splendid body of water, so conducive to contemplation. There is constant change, nearly always movement. Ripples, their edges catching the light, flow, now at speed, now quietly, to the ocean. The tide changes. The waves, usually gentle, head inland. For very brief periods at the turn of the tide a flat calm prevails. Now and then a capricious storm catches my attention.

Seasons on the Arm are reflected in the colour of the water and the wildlife activity: in winter, when few boats disturb the natural movement, ice floes sparkle as they float on the ripples. After a spell of very low temperatures the surface is covered by a thin sheet of ice that can be easily dispersed by the movement of the water.

Wildlife varies according to the time of year. Seagulls, ducks, mergansers, cormorants, loons, oldsquaw, grebe, and occasional seals, all add interest to the view. Best watched early in the morning and at sunset, eagles and ospreys perform dramatic dives, emerging with fish for their young, in nests near the head of the Arm.

Boats of every kind add life in summer and fall: my favourites are the flotillas of sailboats with colourful spinnakers bellying in the wind. At first light, rowers in racing shells speed by, training for the competitions later in the season. In summer the yacht club's motor launch calls at various wharves, picking up its passengers for their daily sailing classes.

Oaklands, a property that once comprised almost a kilometre of waterfront on the Arm, included the land on which our house was built. The name is still reflected in two huge, gnarled oak trees, once actually touching the house, that give shade in summer, and provide food for the squirrels.

The public wharf at the end of Oakland Road is reached by a steep footpath. This is the narrowest and deepest part of the channel. Recent studies by Gordon Fader and colleagues at the Bedford Institute of Oceanography, which were made public in a vivid poster of "seabedscapes" in 2002, have added to our knowledge of the Northwest Arm. Their research revealed the presence of a deep depression in the sea floor. Strong currents have prevented deposits of sediment in this area that they have called a "bottle collector hole." I can picture the underwater site as I watch divers searching for the bottles which have been thrown overboard for the past two hundred years. Sometimes when one of their finds seems exciting, it is worthwhile going down the precipitous walkway to the shore. The divers are always willing to show off their treasures.

A great rock, formerly knows as Tremain's rock, lies beside the public wharf, and used to be a focal point for swimmers. Years ago, before there were properties on the shore, the beach was probably quite wide. Until about fifteen years ago, the water was safe for swimming and we entered the Arm from a ladder at the end of our wharf, not far from the rock. To swim to the Dingle and back was an achievement, although this was forbidden by the Arm Patrol who tried to maintain safety for swimmers and boaters. The water rarely became really warm, but by late summer it seemed pleasant. It is not so long ago that a lifeguard was on duty on one or other of the Dingle beaches every summer. That was reassuring, as the water at those beaches required frequent testing: if a high level of impurity was found, the beach would be closed, and we would abide by the same rules. Sadly, increasing pollution has discouraged such activities, and fewer people are now prepared to immerse themselves in the waters of the Arm.

At one time a shelter for ferry passengers stood beside the public wharf. The boat could be summoned from its base near the Dingle by pressing a buzzer. There were occasions when the ferryman arrived to find no one waiting, although mischievous giggles could be heard coming from further up the hill. In 2002 the ferry resumed service temporarily. Residents on the west side of the Arm appreciated the speedy crossing, with the extra advantage of avoiding rush hour at the Armdale Rotary. Those from the east enjoyed easy access to the Dingle footpaths for a morning walk.

In every season morning and evening, sometimes dodging ice, sometimes heavy traffic, appear two constant users — a work boat and a commuter. Back and forth to the harbour chugs the purposeful blue Cape Island, the Dive Com 3, that is used for commercial diving and marine construction work, and a canoe paddled by a woman who finds this method of travel faster, more convenient, and more fun than driving around the Armdale Rotary. There have been occasions when I have watched with some anxiety until she has reached shore. For recreation, although swimming and skating are less common now, as a channel, and for sheer beauty, few cities have been granted a body of water comparable with the Northwest Arm.

Janet Kitz
May 2003

CHAPTER 1

EARLY SETTLEMENT ON THE NORTHWEST ARM

Looking up the Northwest Arm from the Chain Rock. J.E. Woolford (c. 1818). In the foreground is a ring which anchored a chain boom that closed off the mouth of the Arm.

DEFENDING THE TOWN

This portion of Moses Harris's map of Halifax Harbour shows the Northwest Arm identified as Sandwich or Hawk's River. (1749)

From the time of Samuel de Champlain's voyage to the New World in the early 1600s, both the French and English noted on their maps the peninsula at Chibouctou (present-day Halifax). It was cited as a fine, defensible spot from which to protect the harbour, an excellent site for sheltering a fleet of ships.

The English who first established settlement at Halifax in 1749 mistakenly identified the Northwest Arm as a river. Edward Cornwallis, the town's founder, was pleased to note that Sandwich Point (today's Point Pleasant) was easily defensible. With Hawk's River (also known as Sandwich River) on one side, which he knew to be navigable for at least some distance, he set his men to clearing the point with a view to building a fortified settlement. One of them, perhaps working on the wooded hillside, described the river in a letter home as "about as wide as the Thames at London Bridge."

Cornwallis soon realized that this was, in fact, an inlet, not a river, and that the point was exposed to storms and surrounded by extensive offshore shoals. The townsite was then moved round into the harbour, snug below the drumlin which would soon be crowned by a fort.

The native Mi'kmaq, who were familiar with this body of water, named it Wagwoltichk (end of the bay). Although no evidence has been found of regular summer encampments, such as those found elsewhere around the harbour, the sheltered waters were rich fishing grounds for herring, mackerel, eel and shark. In addition, seals and other mammals were easily hunted along the shore.

The English under Cornwallis's rule were fearful of attack by Mi'kmaq on the land side and French from the ocean. They noted that the isthmus between the head of the Arm and present-day Bedford Basin was sufficiently narrow that the early settlement could be secured from attack by a defensive line. Three palisaded blockhouses were constructed, all linked by a patrolled road. The South Blockhouse overlooked the head of the Arm and the beginning of the Peninsular Road from a spot just above the present railway bridge on Chebucto Road.

There was some concern as the French, already well established at Louisbourg, at the northern tip of Île Royale (present-day Cape Breton), were paying a bounty for English scalps. When three workers at a new sawmill at the mouth of the stream from Indian (Chocolate) Lake, outside the fortified line, were killed in the 1750s, these concerns were increased.

Much of the work on the blockhouses was done by the contingent of European settlers, known as Foreign Protestants, recruited by the British to help build the colony in Nova Scotia. These German-speaking immigrants from the *Gale*, the *Murdoch* and the *Pearl* landed at the isthmus and settled in small log huts close by the blockhouses. Those who owed money for their passage were required to work on the road and fortifications. For some two years there was a

Indians fishing on the Arm. Unknown artist. (1830)

Halifax artist John O'Brien left many views of Halifax harbour. This painting of the Northwest Arm looks down to the harbour mouth from Quinpool Road, at the head of the Arm, showing a variety of boating activity. (1890)

considerable settlement of families as well as single men at the Arm and along the line of the Peninsular Road. Later they were moved to the new settlement of Lunenburg.

Just as the fear of native attack was being laid to rest, the renewed threat of a French invasion arose. Military officials realized they would have to deal with the vulnerable rear of the settlement; a hostile fleet could sail into the Northwest Arm and land an invading force on the peninsula without a shot being fired from the shore.

To counter this, temporary defensive earthworks were placed on Point Pleasant in 1762. Lord Colville, the admiral, ordered a boom of timber and iron chains be placed across the mouth of the Arm, with an armed sloop stationed on guard. The crew, augmented by twenty Newfoundlanders, was issued thirty rounds of grape and round shot and a month's provisions

before they headed off to the Arm for the summer. It was a peaceful tour of duty. No French invasion materialized.

Soon, however, a more immediate threat presented itself. Greatly alarmed by the civil unrest in the colonies to the south, the authorities instituted martial law in Halifax in 1775 and forbade all vessels access to the Arm, except when specifically licensed, such as for fishing.

Military and naval authorities co-operated to keep the defensive forces at peak alert. War games, known as sham fights, were a favourite device and an account of one such occasion survives. On September 30, 1778, at sunrise, a bugle sounded the alarm over the sleeping town. During the night the admiral sailed five warships into the Arm and landed his "invasion force" in the woods of Point Pleasant. Brigadier-General McLean rallied his troops — the Argyle Highlanders, the Edinburgh Regiment, the Duke of Hamilton's Regiment and the Royal Regiment of Artillery — to march on the point and repel the invaders. The woods were cleared by mid-afternoon, the sailors retreating to the western shore of the Arm under cover of the ships. General McLean's attempt to follow up his victory by dislodging the sailors from the woods was something of an anticlimax. He ordered his men to build rafts from timber along the shore. One raft was detached from its towboat and wrecked on the shoals near the point. At once the battle was over, as the admiral's men joined in the rescue of their erstwhile enemies floundering in the harbour.

In 1776, when the unrest culminated in revolution, the crumbling fortifications at the point were reviewed. The two 1762 batteries were reconstructed and three more added, including two on the Arm south of the Chain Rock, but the chain boom itself was not reinstated.

View of the Northwest Arm. Bessie Brown (c. 1890)

J.E. Woolford's view entitled "York Redoubt from the Northwest Arm" shows the house where Joseph Howe, one of Nova Scotia's most famous politicians, was born in 1804. (c.1818)

MELVILLE ISLAND PRISON

Above: Melville Island from the Halifax side. J.E. Woolford. (c. 1818)
Below: Hulks of ships were moored in Bedford Basin and used as prisons in wartime and in peace.

The Napoleonic Wars and continuing struggle between France and Britain for sovereignty in North America brought hundreds of French prisoners to Halifax. They were held on overcrowded prison hulks in Bedford Basin until, in 1803, the Admiralty leased an island at the head of the Arm for a prison. A large wooden barrack and a three-storey officers' house were built and fortified

with a few artillery pieces. The island was renamed Melville Island in honour of Henry Dundas, Viscount Melville, First Lord of the Admiralty. François Bourneuf, wounded aboard the frigate *La Furieuse* in 1809, recorded his impressions of prison life on Melville Island:

When I arrived all the Frenchmen were working. Some were knitting stockings, mitts, gloves, or purses, and some were spinning. . . . Other Frenchmen made hats from birchbark, all kinds of crafts from bones, such as snuff boxes, knives, forks, dice, dominoes. . . .the jailer sold the prisoners bread, butter, potatoes, lime, soap, pepper, thread, needles, tobacco, onions and other necessaries, but he also did the prisoners' shopping in town as required, bringing them. . . more than 5,000 pounds of wool a year.

Painters, jewellers, carpenters, schoolteachers, dancing masters and music masters were all in business at the prison, or in town. "Tailors and shoemakers made goods for Halifax gentlemen," Bourneuf reported. "A number of prisoners went out to work as domestics for households in Halifax; and masons plied their trade, making stone walls around the gardens of houses between the prison and the city."

Many prisoners kept animals as pets. Hens were housed in stone coops in the prison yard and their eggs were sold in the city. Other prisoners sold butter and candy, as well as cod and mackerel caught in the Arm.

Going drinking with the guards at a nearby mill was also a popular pastime. Sometimes this ended in escape, although, as Bourneuf pointed out, "Some had been [at Halifax] for a long time. They liked it because they were well paid and well fed. A few inmates took a great deal of money back to France."

For American prisoners in the War of 1812 conditions were somewhat different because of overcrowding. The prisoners' hammocks hung in tiers by night and were taken down by day. Playing cards or planning elaborate escape attempts were popular pastimes for the inmates, the majority of whom were privateers' crews — young men from New England seaports, many with relatives in Nova Scotia. They were justifiably indignant at the treatment they received at British hands.

Herbert Grey Austen, a military artist, painted several views of the area, including this one entitled "Crossing the Arm" (c. 1847)

Melville Island prison about 100 years after it was first put to use.

Benjamin Waterhouse of Massachusetts was the surgeon on a captured American privateer. When he arrived at Melville Island in May 1813, he recorded: "I had time to notice the occupations of these poor fellows. Some were washing their own clothes; others mending them. Others were intent on ridding their shirts and other clothing from lice, which to the disgrace of the British government, are allowed to infest our prisoners."

Waterhouse conceded that the buildings, all of which were painted red, had a neat appearance, but found the country bleak: the Arm presented "a range of dreary hills on the northern side [with] a few scattered dwellings, and some attempts at cultivation; on the southern nothing appears but immense piles of rocks, with bushes, scattered here and there, in their hollows and crevices."

There were about 900 prisoners at Melville Island when Waterhouse arrived, but "many died by the severity of the winter; for the quantity of fuel allowed…was insufficient to convey warmth through the prison. The men were cruelly harassed by the barbarous custom of mustering and parading them in the severest cold, and even in snow storms."

The young surgeon was appalled by the condition of a group of American prisoners who arrived at Melville Island after being marched from Upper Canada to Quebec, and then "crowded … on board transports, like negroes in a guinea ship, where some suffered death, and others merely escaped it… The treatment of these poor fellows…was barbarous in the extreme, and highly disgraceful to the British name and nation."

View of the prison from the ferry, at the foot of today's Jubilee Road. J.E. Woolford (c. 1818)

View of Melville Island and Deadman's Island (right) where prisoners were interred.

Prisoners died by the hundreds at Melville Island, mostly during epidemics of pneumonia, typhoid fever and dysentery – the result of overcrowding. They were buried nearby at Deadman's Island.

On June 4, 1814, American privateer Benjamin Franklin Palmer, of Stonington, Connecticut recorded in his diary; "Four prisoners carried to Target Hill this morning, a place where they bury the dead. I'm fearful a number of us will visit that place this summer if not released."

After the American prisoners were freed, the prison became refugee housing. Near the end of the war British ships carrying refugees seeking freedom from slavery began arriving from the Chesapeake Bay area.

These refugees were inadequately clothed and completely unprepared for the Nova Scotian climate. To add to their misery, smallpox broke out in the spring of 1815. The refugees were first vaccinated, then issued the warm woolen uniforms of captured American and demobilized British soldiers and they were quartered at the empty Melville Island prison, hastily refurbished with whitewash and new windows. There they remained until land grants could be arranged.

Most of the refugees were eventually given land at Beech Hill (now Beechville) but a few families settled at the head of the Arm, in the vicinity of today's St. Margarets Bay Road.

The island prison was used as a quarantine hospital for typhus victims in 1847. For the rest of the nineteenth century it served as a military prison.

THE WESTERN SHORE

View from Cowie's Hill on the western shore of the Northwest Arm. George Isham Parkyns (1801)

Captain William Spry, who served at Louisbourg and Quebec, was posted to Halifax as the chief engineer and army surveyor in 1769. Like many other military and colonial officials, he welcomed the opportunity to acquire land grants, developing them to meet the needs of the growing colony, as well as for personal profit.

When he first arrived in Halifax, Spry acquired 200 hectares of land, about eight kilometres from the Arm in the present-day Spryfield area. He then built a new road to reach this land before petitioning for a grant of an additional 400 hectares, with the object of settling tenant farmers there. In 1783, when he returned to England, there were between 32 and 40 hectares of cleared upland on his Spryfield farm, supporting about 30 head of cattle, poultry, an established orchard, vegetable gardens, several houses, two barns and a stable.

In order to get all this valuable produce to market, much of it had to be carried over granite outcrops, through bogs and down precipitous slopes above Cowies Cove before reaching the bridge at the head of the Arm. Petitions from many outlying areas were addressed to the Legislature over the years, pleading for assistance in filling in ruts, mending bridges, clearing stones and trimming back the undergrowth which threatened to close the roads entirely, but in general, responsibility for upkeep rested with the users.

It was a fisherman, James Williams, who introduced a new level of settlement to the area when he became a highly effective land speculator in partnership with his son-in-law, George Castaffin. Williams fished from an eastern-shore lot he bought in 1778, but in 1780 he also acquired lands on the opposite shore. Purchasing the adjoining 80-hectare farm grants of Daniel Hill and Thomas Bridge, Williams and Castaffin held all the shoreline from the quarry lots at today's Purcells Cove to the narrows at the Dingle. Four years later, they sold the entire 160 hectares to George McIntosh, a merchant and speculator.

Quarries close to the shore of the Arm were an excellent source of the ironstone, granite and slate needed in the construction of roads and forts around the harbour. At first the army used quarries at Chebucto Head and Sambro and, until in 1815 John Trider's quarries, near Purcells Cove, caught the military's attention. Lt. Col. Wright, in charge of completing Sherbrooke Tower on McNab's Island, reported using good quality granite from this source. Granite and ironstone from the Queen's Quarry and slate from the nearby King's Quarry were used for the major reconstruction of the Citadel in 1828.

The military used Trider's stone roads and facilities but his quarries were taken over by the authorities. All

The military used quarries on the western shore to build roads and fortifications around the harbour, including Prince of Wales Tower, Point Pleasant.

land grants contained the proviso that should the property be required for government purposes, the grantee would have to hand over the land, receiving compensation for any improvements made.

When the era of large government works drew to a close, the quarries returned to private hands, and quarrying became a good source of income for landowners along the western shore. Families like the Slaunwhites and the Yeadons became skilled stonecutters, renowned for their ability to read the fissures in the rock so accurately that when the stone hammer fell, in the words of one observer, "the rocks sliced like cheese."

Dozens of small informal quarries pitted the rocky western slopes of the Arm and the barrens beyond. When, in 1860, William Pryor was selling the 20-hectare lot behind Miles Cove, at the Dingle, one of the advantages he pointed out was that it had "every facility for furnishing large quantities of building stone." Stone quarried behind Williams Lake might be brought out along a quarry road or across the ice to the stone road which led from the shore of the lake straight down through today's Boulderwood to the Arm. A few dressed stones still lie where they fell into the clear waters of the lake. Once at the Arm the quarried slabs were loaded onto boats or barges.

William Eagar's 1839 view looks across to mills and farmland on the western shore

MILLS

View of Hosterman's Mills by J.E. Woolford c. 1818.

Halifax was considered by the military to have a fine harbour but the worst soil on the whole southern coast. There were a few pockets of good land on the uplands of the peninsula but most grain had to be imported from more fertile areas like Lunenburg and the Annapolis Valley, to be ground in mills on the western shore of the Arm. The streams that coursed down the rocky hillside from Indian Lake and Williams Lake provided power for two mills.

George McIntosh, who had amassed a lot of land on the western side of the Arm, most of which he divided and sold off in 20-hectare parcels, retained 180 hectares surrounding the stream flowing from Williams Lake. There he went into partnership with William Cochrane, building a grist mill and a substantial farmhouse for the resident miller and his family. The Mill Farm was leased until 1811, when it was sold to Loyalist Robert Letson. Still later it was operated by Richard Dingle, the Hanleys and finally the Lawson family, who called it Sandwich Mills, and at various times manufactured superfine flour, beer and nails on the site.

The most northerly of the western shore streams had been exploited since the eighteenth century, first

Thomas Hosterman's house at Melville Cove in 1936.

by a sawmill, then a mill for cocoa beans. In 1788 a German immigrant, John Hosterman, leased the land where the chocolate mill had stood and set up a grist mill, with the grain being brought in by water. In the 1820s Hosterman's son Thomas, with his brother-in-law William Black and William's brother Samuel upgraded the family grist until they had four pairs of grind stones, a barley mill, fans and a wheat-cleaning machine, all driven by a new overshot waterwheel. The mill was described as the largest undertaking of its kind in the province.

The Hosterman property also accommodated a snuff mill operated by Joseph Austen, who was in the tobacco business in Halifax. In 1831, Austen advertised a complete repair and upgrade of his premises. Taking snuff was popular in the early part of the nineteenth century, and Austen claimed that he manufactured and

Edward John Russell's 1872 view includes many of the activities that have shaped the Arm today. While picknickers are preparing to enjoy themselves around the ruins of a fort – Chain Rock Battery, a good sized sailing vessel is heading out to sea, having perhaps called in at the mills visible on the western shore. Close to shore are some fishermen in a small boat.

sold a very superior quality, both wholesale and retail.

By 1835, not only tobacco and grain were being unloaded at Hosterman's Mills. Entrepreneurs Johns and Suttie operated the Halifax Foundry on this site, where they paid high prices for copper, brass, pewter and old iron. This scrap metal was transformed into numerous articles either from the customer's own patterns or ones they would make on site. Available at the foundry, or from the agent in town, were patent windlasses, sheaves, Franklin stoves, mill cranes and ovens of various sizes. Waterwheels were used in iron foundries to drive the bellows that kept the furnaces going. Johns and Suttie, who were producing wrought iron work of all kinds, may have employed a similar mechanical arrangement to power a trip hammer to pound and shape the raw iron.

By 1862, Thomas Hosterman's sons, John and Charles, were operating the factory complex, which now employed 40 men, and were contemplating major investments in new machinery. Charles, in partnership with William Cooper, was running the Melville Iron Foundry in the shell of the old stone mill. The foundry consumed over 270 tonnes tons of Pictou coal a year and its agents bought scrap iron from all over the province. Several overshot wheels, the largest about seven metres in diameter, were set at various levels in the stream, producing some 35 horsepower to drive the machinery within for rolling, cutting and trimming the iron. The foundry's two furnaces, for puddling, bailing and annealing the iron, were in the lowest level of the mill. Other levels of the foundry contained casting and finishing rooms. Farther up the hill, John operated nail factory, where sheet iron from the foundry was cut into various sizes of nails and spikes.

When Thomas died in 1863, he left his large house to John, his eldest son, but the Hosterman enterprises had large debts which jeopardized all the industry on the stream. A series of court actions concerning these the debts forced the sale of most of the Hosterman holdings in 1866. Only the nail factory was still in operation by the 1870s.

Several other small industries also operated here in the 1870s, including a brush factory in one of the Hosterman buildings, a box factory and the Chandler Electric Light Company, which generated electricity for the town and was briefly located at the mouth of the stream.

In 1879, the old mill came into the hands of the Henderson and Potts paint company which manufactured "iron clad" roofing paint, white lead and zinc paint as well as 16 shades of their own Handy Colours brand. These extremely flammable materials resulted in a disastrous fire in 1887. The factory was destroyed, and Henderson and Potts was forced to move to the north end of Halifax. In 1899 the company bought a piece of Hosterman land beside the old paint wharf for a barytes mill which remained in operation for about 20 years.

Mills at the head of the Arm. Michael Seymour (1845)

THE PENITENTIARY

The New York state prison at Auburn, on which the penitentiary system in Halifax was modelled.

An isolated stretch of shore near Point Pleasant was selected in the 1840s as an ideal site for a provincial penitentiary. The institution, designed to run on a system developed at the state prison in Auburn, New York, replaced the overcrowded and dilapidated Bridewell on Spring Garden Road. It incorporated training in trades, such as shoemaking and stone-cutting. Many of the guards were instructors in trades, and the male prisoners, some as young as 12 years old, worked in the tailor's, shoemaker's or blacksmith's shops, or the broom store. Others were trained in stone-cutting, a trade which they practised while completing the walls of the penitentiary.

The government purchased two of Trider's small quarries for the stone to build the penitentiary. Plans show a three-storey stone structure. The women, usually very few in number, were strictly segregated from the men in a small cell block with their own exercise yard. A nursery was included in the plan, because women sometimes gave birth in the penitentiary. Their days were occupied with spinning, knitting and washing doing laundry, under the charge of the Matron (usually the governor's wife).

Discipline for all inmates varied, depending upon the inclination of the governor and whether or not political patronage interfered with his authority over the guards. Prisoners were not usually chained, unless they were considered a danger to others. The usual punishment for rule infractions was solitary confinement in one of three "dark cells."

The prison diet was substantial but monotonous: porridge, molasses, bread or hard biscuits and soup filled with vegetables grown in the prison garden. Fish or meat was sometimes added. Water was drawn from a well in the prison yard but by the 1860s the supply had become inadequate, and in summer the prison drinking water had to be brought over the Arm in barrels from Williams Lake.

Escapes from the penitentiary were quite frequent — the neighbouring houses were warned to watch their boats when prisoners got away after one incident in which six convicts stole a small boat from Colonel Sawyer at Bilton. One prisoner is reputed to have swam the Arm to freedom, hiding in the barrens behind Williams Lake (or, some say, the quarries), where he was secretly fed by sympathetic local residents until he could get away. In 1850, a particularly daring group made off in landowner Henry Lawson's schooner from the mill cove wharf, and managed to stay away for 24 days. Lawson demanded compensation from the House of Assembly for his vessel's time lost.

In 1864 the Board of Works recommended to the House of Assembly that all prisoners be photographed "in order to facilitate the identification of confirmed evil doers" but, like many of the board's ideas, this one does not seem to have been acted upon.

When Nova Scotia joined Confederation in 1867, a Canadian inspector was sent down to make a report on the two Maritime penitentiaries. Local officials were taken aback to discover that he considered the prison at the Arm to be the worst managed of any in the new Dominion.

Convicts sauntered up and down prison corridors, smoking and chatting. If they went to their cells, it was to read, or whittle wood. "Between keepers and convicts there was the most perfect good fellowship," the inspector was reported to have said. "The cells, corridors, yard and workshops were all filthy." This "fellowship" had not precluded violent confrontations; a riot had broken out shortly before the inspector's visit. The guards, with an annual salary of $400, were described by one newspaper reporter, trying to account for the uprising, as "a force of antiquated keepers who are scarcely able to move about themselves much less guard others."

Immediately after the inspector's visit reforms were put in place. The guards were ordered to wash themselves and told that ragged and dirty uniforms would no longer be tolerated. Quantities of soap and water were provided and the convicts were put to work cleaning the building and their cells.

The prison at the Arm was vacated in 1880 when

The three-storey penitentiary building at the time of its partial demolition and conversion to a gas factory.

the new Dominion Penitentiary at Dorchester, New Brunswick, began to take convicted criminals from all the Maritime provinces. On a July morning the inmates from the Halifax prison, perhaps looking forward to a change of scene and a rail journey on a beautiful summer day, were mustered and lectured on good behaviour. Then, dressed in yellow and black prison uniforms, their hair cropped and their underwear marked so they could be instantly identified, 58 male prisoners were manacled two by two and driven by wagon to the North Street Depot. The only two women prisoners were left behind and it was expected that they would soon be pardoned.

The institution remained deserted for the next two years. Then, after the terrible Poor House fire of 1882, it was fitted out with bedding and stoves so that the survivors could move in. They stayed there for four years until the Poor Asylum on South Street was rebuilt.

Above: Site plan for the penitentiary.
Right: Nineteenth-century engravings of the new prisons give an idealistic view of the conditions. The Halifax penitentiary had very small prison cells and, according to inspectors, disorderly management.

CHAPTER 2

COUNTRY ESTATES

Thornvale

STUDLEY

View of the Shore near Point Pleasant. Alexander Croke (c. 1810)

Studley was the imposing estate of Judge Alexander Croke, who was described by a contemporary as "an able though rather unpopular character." He presided over the Court of Vice Admiralty, which spent much of its time during the Napoleonic wars auctioning off the lucrative naval prizes brought in to Halifax by privateers. At home, he relaxed by composing scathing satirical verse lampooning almost everyone in society — other Council members, their wives, even the stately Bishop Inglis. Croke sat on the Executive Council and acted briefly as administrator of the province during the governor's absence, making him one of the most influential and powerful people in the colony.

Studley was a delightful family house, with eleven rooms and a large garret, perched on the rocky pine-clad hillside looking out towards the mouth of the Arm. A sloping drive, lined with willows and oaks, led down from the Studley Road and across a little brook before approaching the house. The coach house had stabling for four horses and could hold three or four carriages. Walks were laid out through the woods to take advantage of the most picturesque views, and Croke himself retired to write in a secluded bower overlooking the Arm, which he called the Temple of Peace.

Studley's 16 hectares operated as a self-sufficient year-round estate, with sheltered walls for growing fruit, a garden under cultivation, cows, pigs and poultry, a dairy, a root cellar, beer and wine cellars and cistern for storing large quantities of rainwater.

In 1816, Alexander Croke put the Studley estate on the market and left for England. George McIntosh's daughter and son-in-law, Louisa and Matthew Richardson, bought it and moved there with their family in 1820. Stretching from the heights of the peninsula to the shores of the Arm, Studley was one of Halifax's most beautiful properties, although even this may have been cold comfort for as Croke complained:

> As drizly vapours, up Chebucto bay,
> From banks of cod fish, wind their creeping way;
> Each narrow chink, the piercing fog pervades;
> And flannel scarcely guards the Shivering Maids.

Perhaps enthusiastic stoking of the Studley fireplaces was the cause of the chimney fire that destroyed the house in February 1831. The Richardsons built a new and elegantly proportioned Studley on the same site the following year. They offered a corner of the property to a group of keen quoits players who set up the Studley Quoit Club in 1858.

Left: Alexander Croke

Below: The Studley Quoit Club moved to a corner of the Studley property in 1858. It was a popular club for an exclusively male membership.

Matthew died in 1860 and Louisa remained there until her death in 1867. The property came into the hands of Antoinette Nordbeck, daughter of a renowned local silversmith. She lived there with her friends, Reverend Robert Murray (editor of the outspoken denominational newspaper the *Presbyterian Witness*) and his wife Elizabeth, and she bequeathed the house to them on her death. It became known as the Murray homestead when it was sold to Dalhousie University in 1912. The house was demolished in 1949 to make way for the Arts and Administration building. The willows and oaks lining the original carriageway were cut down and the brook was filled in but even today, the remains of the dry-stone walls along Oxford, Coburg and South Streets are visible, bounding Kings College and Dalhousie as they did Croke's Studley when the fields were first cleared 200 years ago.

The Murray Homestead, which was razed in 1949 during expansion of Dalhousie University, was captured in watercolour by Nova Scotia artist Ruth Wainwright.

BELMONT AND WINWICK

Belmont, rebuilt in the 1850s.

Captain Henry Duncan, Commissioner of the Dockyard and a member of the governing council, built Belmont in about 1790, naming the estate after his family home in Scotland. Known widely as Commissioner's Farm, it was likely run as a self-sufficient estate. The house was all but destroyed by fire in 1811. However, John Howe Jr. bought it and rebuilt it in 1811 and stayed there until his death in 1842. Like many land-owners along the Arm, Howe permitted the public use of his grounds as long as it did not interfere with his privacy or principles. In 1837 the Union Engine Company held its annual August picnic at Belmont. The party departed from the steamboat wharf on the ferry *Sir Charles Ogle*, which brought them down the harbour and round into the Arm. A band played and members danced on the deck. The day passed with a picnic held on the grounds of Belmont and more cruising, music and dancing among the "sylvan scenes of the Arm" until at last, at about 8 o'clock, the whole party walked back to town, with the band playing a popular march.

The property passed through the hands of William Clarke to J. Scott Tremain (a nephew of Richard Tremain who had built nearby Oakland), whose first intention was to divide the 37 hectares into "village lots." In the end he decided simply to keep the lands and to commission a new house in the latest "cottage" style, from the fashionable architect and builder Henry G. Hill.

Tremain did not live long enough to enjoy his new Belmont. In 1856, his executors put the whole estate on the market. At the time about 14 hectares were cultivated, including pasture and a fine growth of mixed woodlands, all surrounded by a substantial

Left: Eliza Ritchie, professor and Dean of Women at Dalhousie University, lived at Winwick.
Cemtre: Painting by an unknown artist of the shore at Winwick
Below: The ferry Sir Charles Ogle brought people from the town to Winwick for walks and picnics.

stone wall. There were several farm workers' houses which the executors proposed could easily be converted into summer residences. The whole estate was sold to Judge John W. Ritchie, Nova Scotia's Solicitor General from 1864 to 1867. He was among those who attended the London Conference which drafted the British North America Act, defining the terms of Confederation. He was made a senator in 1867 and lived at Belmont until his death in 1890.

Ritchie's son Thomas lived with his family in the main house, while his brother George, a lawyer and vice-president of the Royal Bank, and his sisters Eliza and Ella, built their own house, Winwick, in the grounds. It is noteworthy that Eliza, a professor of Sanskrit at Dalhousie University, became the Dean of Women in 1912 and was the first woman to serve on the university's board of governors.

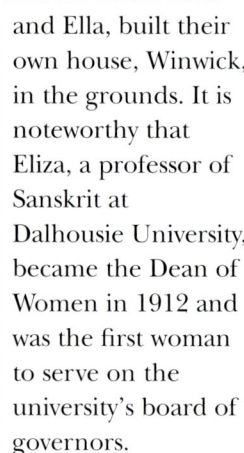

Winwick burned to the ground in 1917 (the revenge, it was rumoured, of a disgruntled coachman), and the property was sold. Several years later, a Halifax councillor, John J. Hines, decided to rebuild the house. After reassembling much of the original land, Hines imported ship's carpenters from Lunenburg to build a house in keeping with the magnificent setting, designed in the latest "bungalow" style. It was sold to Premier Angus L. Macdonald in 1938 and remained in the MacDonald family for the next 40 years despite a proposal that it become the premiers' official residence.

Belmont itself stood until 1964, when it was razed for the new housing development, Belmont-on-the-Arm.

OAKLANDS

Oaklands, built by William Cunard, son of shipping magnate Samuel Cunard

Richard Tremain's house, Oakland, burned in 1848, leaving its memory in the name of Oakland Road. The next owner of his land, William Cunard, son of shipping magnate Sir Samuel Cunard, transformed the property, acquiring more land and commissioning a new house, Oaklands. Designed by Halifax architects Henry Elliot and Henry Frederick Busch and completed in 1864 it was built of Philadelphia pressed brick with a granite foundation and freestone trimming; ironwork was imported from Scotland for the balconies and verandahs, and many interior fittings came from the United States. The spacious rooms were finished in black walnut and birch. No expense was spared.

Cunard's lands ran from the shore to Robie Street, where an imposing Gothic porter's lodge guarded the entrance to the property. Wrought-iron gates opened onto a tree-lined drive that curved down through the fields and woods ending in a circular drive in front of the new house.

The estate became the scene of many agricultural innovations. Oaklands' outdoor staff was headed by the redoubtable Scottish gardener, Alexander Fleming, who kept the parterres filled with bedding plants. Figs, strawberries, tomatoes and many varieties of grapes were successfully cultivated in the glasshouses. Rare breeds of cattle and poultry were imported from Britain and Cunard won prizes for butter, milk and

Left: Philip Carteret Hill, premier of Nova Scotia
Below: The railway cutting sliced through the old Oaklands estate.

Fleming's expertise with grapes was soon winning prizes at the agricultural shows. The vinery was now equipped to produce two and a quarter tonnes in a season, and the first large-scale export of Nova Scotia grapes was shipped to the United States from Oaklands in 1873. The varieties grown included Black Hamburg, with clusters weighing up to one kilogram, Black Alicane and Muscat.

Mrs. Hill, however, managed to incense Mr. Fleming by sending a servant to the vinery to cut a bunch of grapes, which she wished to give to an ailing friend. After venting his fury, Fleming was dismissed.

He refused to go. For weeks he would not vacate the gardener's cottage. Hill had its doors and windows removed, whereupon Fleming accused the carpenters of assaulting his wife. Finally the matter arrived in magistrate's court before the embarrassed Henry Pryor, a neighbour. The *Acadian Recorder* described the case in detail as a "disgraceful squabble" and eventually it was dismissed.

After Hill's defeat in the provincial elections of 1878, he and his wife decided to spend their declining years in England. Princess Louise took time from her busy schedule to view Oaklands, considering it as a possible summer residence during her husband's tour of duty as governor general. Instead, however, Oaklands became the home of Lord Alexander Russell, C.B., the lieutenant-general commanding Her Majesty's forces in Canada.

cheese at the Industrial and Agricultural Exhibition, demonstrating the effect of breeding on dairy products. The *British Colonist* praised him for "taking an interest in agricultural pursuits as a relaxation from the cares of the counting house."

After the death of his elder brother Edward, William Cunard was required in Britain to take charge of the Cunard Line's affairs. Philip Carteret Hill (who would soon become the premier of Nova Scotia) and his family became Oaklands' new tenants.

The Hills kept Fleming on, intending to continue Oaklands' established horticultural traditions.

In 1906 Oaklands was sold to Roderick Macdonald, a keen supporter of the Halifax Amateur Boating Club. He built a large boathouse, and permitted the club to use it. He kept the property until 1914, when the Ocean Terminals project began, and the projected route placed Oaklands squarely in the middle of the railway right of way. F.B. McCurdy bought Oaklands and arranged for the house to be taken to a new site. On the night of December 28, 1914, however, as it was perched on giant steel girders, waiting to be moved, fire broke out and raced through the building, reducing it to rubble.

THE BOWER

The Bower in 1860 (above), and today (below).

The Bower was built by John Halliburton, a surgeon and Rhode Island Loyalist, who became head of the Royal Navy's medical department in Halifax. In 1806 he purchased the land from James Williams and his sons-in-law, George Castaffin and William Peck, and probably built the simple pitch-roofed cottage soon after.

The Bower became the summer home of Brenton Halliburton, Chief Justice of Nova Scotia, who added the library wing and perhaps was responsible for the Victorian remodelling of the house. In the latter part of the nineteenth century the windows were enlarged and the roof changed to a combination of mansard and hip-gable to give more space and light on the upper floor.

In the early twentieth century the house belonged to W.B.A. Ritchie, a lawyer, whose cousins lived at Belmont and Winwick. Ritchie's son Charles, a diarist and diplomat, was born at the Bower in 1906.

When Charles Ritchie revisited the Bower in the 1930s, long after it had been sold, he described the changes that so disturbed him. The curving drive with its entrance gateposts and lodge had disappeared and a new cul-de-sac, which followed a different alignment, left the house at an awkward angle. The arching trees beside the drive and the woods had been felled to make way for suburban bungalows; the Virginia creeper that covered the dark red shingled walls had been cut down, and the house was repainted a pale yellow. All that remained of the lawns and gardens was the old oak tree which stood on a patch of grass.

BIRCHAM, BLOOMINGDALE AND FAIRFIELD

Alfred Gilpin Jones and his wife in front of their home, Bloomingdale.

When William Pryor Sr. died in 1859, and his sons began to divide some of the Pryor holdings, three brothers-in-law, John Stairs, Robert Morrow and Alfred Gilpin Jones, bought Pryor properties on either side of Coburg Road. They were further linked by the family business, William Stairs, Son and Morrow. The three families proceeded to develop elaborate estates on the shores of the Northwest Arm where they keenly pursued amateur careers in horticulture and the sciences.

To the south of Coburg Road, Robert Morrow Jr. and his wife Helen Stairs built the extravagant

Bircham. Their granddaughter, Marjorie Morrow, described the property as she remembered it:

> The foundation of the cellar had French clay around it for two feet and for a depth of two feet below the foundation. Every bit of the beautiful woodwork was handcarved and all the hardwood was of solid brass imported from England expressly for use in the house. Throughout the property there were French drains cut out of the solid rock, some of them large enough for a man to get through. There were fully 600 trees, of which more than 400 were imported from various countries — creeping pines from Norway, silver birches from Scotland, which gave the estate its name, and in particular, some beautiful purple beeches.

Just as his father had been interested in shells, corals and geology, Robert Morrow Jr., in turn, took up the study of marine biology. Fishermen brought live specimens to the servants' entrance of Bircham, whence they were transferred to a saltwater aquarium in the basement for study. Scientific papers issued from Morrow's laboratory, while a paper on Greenland and Vinland, read before the Literary and Historical Society of

At the Piano. Frances M. Jones (1882)

Halifax in 1865, was sufficient to admit him to the Copenhagen Society of Northern Antiquarians.

Across the road, his brother-in-law, Alfred Gilpin Jones built Bloomingdale. There was friendly horti-

Alfred Gilpin Jones, Lieutenant-Governor of Nova Scotia.

cultural rivalry among the neighbours for years, the results of which are still evident. Jones specialized in trees, especially evergreens, while Stairs, at Fairfield, devoted more time to flowering shrubs. The Bloomingdale estate, now the home of the Waegwoltic Club, still boasts a 9-metre high *Kalmia latifolia*, a *Pieris japonica*, magnificent rhododendrons and a weeping Camperdown elm, all planted in the last century.

Jones, like many other Nova Scotia merchants, was opposed to Confederation, but he nonetheless served as MP for Halifax in the first federal Cabinet. He lived at Bloomingdale throughout his lengthy political career, and used the property for entertaining on almost any pretext.

The talented children of the Jones-Stairs-Morrow families, who spent much of their youth at the Arm properties, achieved considerable renown in their later years. Alice Jones became a well-known novelist while her sister Frances became an artist of international distinction.

Just north of Bloomingdale lay Fairfield, home of John Stairs. Perhaps the best known of all the cousins was Stairs' son, Captain William Stairs, the African

explorer, who accompanied Henry Stanley on the expedition to rescue Emin Pasha in 1887-89. Emin Pasha (born Edward Schnitzer) was the Turkish governor of Equatoria, the southernmost province of Sudan, in 1881 when a jihad was launched by Mohammed Ahmed al Mahdi. The uprising drove the Turkish administration out of Sudan, but Emin Pasha was hardly in need of rescue, even when Stanley and Stairs arrived.

Stairs kept a diary during his arduous journeys in Africa. His thoughts often drifted back to his old home on the Arm, especially after he heard of his father's death, and feared that Fairfield might be sold:

> Shall I never again roam about the old place and potter about among the boats down at the shore? Shall we never have any more pleasant evenings together near the bathing house? The brightest thing I always had to look back to when far away from home and the place I always delighted to return to was Fairfield. Shall I never go back there again among the brown birches and spruce trees, back by the side of the dear old Arm, back to the old places of our younger days? How many times have I started away from the old place with a well-loaded basket, off to the woods . . . trout fishing.

Stairs did see his old home again in the following year, 1890. After the successful conclusion of the Emin Pasha expedition he returned to Nova Scotia to spend the summer at Fairfield, and was accorded an unprecedented welcome. The properties along the Arm were illuminated along both shores with bonfires, coloured lights and Chinese lanterns. His relatives at Fairfield, Bloomingdale and Bircham, as well as friends and neighbours at the Lodge, Thornvale and Boscobel all took part. At Hillside electric lamps were used to spell out "Stairs" beside the water. Yachts from the Royal Nova Scotia Yacht Squadron were moored at intervals along the shore, while boats and steamers strung with lights took part in the tribute to the young hero who had grown up on the Arm.

Fairfield was sold first to James Fraser, and then to Saint Mary's Total Abstinence and Benefit Society, which operated it as a social club, Saint Mary's Villa. The house was demolished, and in 1931 replaced by Villa Maria, designed by Andrew Cobb as a residence for the Roman Catholic archbishops. In 2002 when the Waegwoltic Club expanded its facilities, Villa Maria fell to the wrecker's ball.

Captain William G. Stairs

Fairfield

The Conservatory. Frances M. Jones (1883)

MAPLEWOOD

Maplewood, built in 1870.

Maplewood stood on a portion of the Halliburton land. William Almon Hare, a merchant, built the house and passed it soon afterwards to a relative, Mather Byles Almon Jr. who put the property on the market but failed to attract buyers so he took steps to make it pay. For more than two decades Maplewood, with its fourteen rooms, kitchens and pantries, hot and cold water pipes, attractive waterfront location and conservatory, was leased for receptions, balls and parties of all kinds. The Philadelphia and Canadian cricket teams, in Halifax for an important match, were taken for a sail up the Arm by members of the Royal Halifax Yacht Club, and then received at Maplewood.

For five years, from 1878 to 1883, the army rented the house as a residence for senior officers, and as a

The woodlands at Maplewood were popular for Sunday walks.

result it was the scene of some of the most glittering events in Halifax's social calendar. It was during this period, in 1881, that Oscar Wilde came to Halifax to lecture the Academy of Music at the start of his American tour. The *Presbyterian Witness* declared that Wilde was "not a decent associate in any society" but this deterred neither the crowds of fashionable Haligonians who packed the auditorium for two nights, nor General MacDougall, who invited him to dinner at Maplewood.

In the 1880s Almon turned Maplewood over to the managers of the Queen Hotel on Hollis Street, who launched an ambitious and expensive plan to turn the house into a summer hotel. It is not clear why the plan did not succeed, but in the 1890s Maplewood was once again being rented out for parties.

The house was transformed yet again, although briefly, when Governor General Lord Aberdeen and his wife stayed there in August 1894. Lady Aberdeen

Maplewood was rebuilt by David MacKeen (above).

Maplewood had a ballroom with an excellent dance floor. This is a composite photo of a costume ball at the house.

loved Halifax and found Maplewood to be a much nicer house than she had expected, despite its limited accommodations for their entourage. The governor general's aides-de-camp used a tent on the lawn as a sitting room, and were forced to spend the nights at Pine Hill College. A temporary addition to the dining room was needed for the vice-regal dinner parties.

After their Excellencies returned to Ottawa, the furniture purchased for their visit was auctioned off, but before it was removed, local socialites Mrs. Morrow and Mrs. J.F. Kenny held balls at Maplewood. The dance floor was considered to be one of the best in Halifax and "Lady Jane," in her column in the *Acadian Recorder,* confessed that "the anteroom to the

ballroom, being two or three steps higher than the latter itself, gives a delightful view of dances, frocks and (alas!) flirtations."

In 1896 Maplewood was sold to Senator David MacKeen, a director of the People's Heat and Light Company. Mrs. MacKeen is supposed to have found the house impossibly old-fashioned, despite its wonderful dance floor, and persuaded her husband to demolish it and build upon the old foundations a modern house in the Tuscan villa style.

The redesigned Maplewood remained in the MacKeen family until 1974 when it burned to the ground just after the property had been sold for redevelopment.

EMSCOTE

Francklyn family wedding on the steps of Emscote.

Emscote lay just north of the old penitentiary, on land that was part of the Williams and Castaffin grant. This was the site of John Howe's cottage, birthplace of Joseph Howe, one of Nova Scotia's most renowned politicians. In 1864 William Cunard had just built his new Oaklands, and took the chance to buy a nearby property for his sister Sarah Jane and her husband, Colonel Gilbert W. Francklyn. The Francklyns called their new house Emscote, for the English village in Warwickshire close to Colonel Francklyn's former home.

In 1881, they conveyed the property to their son, George E. Francklyn, president of the Halifax branch of his grandfather's firm, S. Cunard and Company. Within a few years the abandoned penitentiary building next door was selected as the site for a new gasworks. The People's Heat and Light Company announced its plans in 1895, with B.F. Pearson, lawyer, entrepreneur and publisher of the *Morning Chronicle* and the *Daily Echo*, at the helm.

The company was hoping to create profit from the by-products of the coking ovens as well as from the sale

Emscote, built on the site of John Howe's cottage.

of the gas, so would be storing materials such as coal tar, sulphate of ammonia, sulphuric acid, benzol and potassic ferrocyanide, in this developing residential area.

Many people were unhappy at the thought of a gasworks, no matter how innovative, on the beautiful waters of the Arm. Letters to the newspapers and to the government deplored the desecration of the Arm, where fumes borne on the prevailing westerly winds would undoubtedly damage trees and vegetation in Point Pleasant Park, as well as on private estates.

George E. Francklyn tried to dissuade company promoters by offering them a piece of Cunard land on Bedford Basin, close to the railway and for half the price, but to no avail. Francklyn then made an arrangement

People's Heat and Light, the gas factory, emitted noxious fumes that forced that Francklyns to leave Emscote.

with the Anglican Church to purchase the property himself for $20,000, only to find that Pearson had outbid him. Pearson's deal was quickly closed, $22,500 changed hands, and renovations to the building began.

Once the gasworks began operating late in 1896, Francklyn's worst fears were realized. Foul-smelling drainage and scum continually entered the waters of the Arm and, as predicted, the gas fumes were beginning to kill trees at Emscote and in Point Pleasant Park.

Emscote was frequently enveloped in dark smoke from the gasworks chimney, or surrounded by a pale blue sulphurous haze. The smell of the fumes made it impossible to sleep with the windows open, and members of the family and staff began to develop boils, skin afflictions, and nose and throat irritations. Ella Abbott, a neighbour at Pine Cottage, at first noted only the disagreeable odours near Emscote, but then her family too broke out in boils; doctors put it down to blood poisoning from the gasworks fumes.

Frances Casten, daughter-in-law of George E. Francklyn, was severely affected by the fumes of the neighbouring gas factory.

Francklyn won an injunction to stop the gasworks operations, but not until he and his family had been driven to leave Emscote permanently. The People's Heat and Light Company was insolvent by 1902, and Pearson, whose intransigence had caused the whole unpleasant episode, became the new owner of Emscote, although at a price widely rumoured to be well above its market value.

Pearson's daughter Florence married F.B. McCurdy, an up-and-coming young stockbroker, and the couple moved into Emscote in the 1920s. The house remained in the family until McCurdy's death in the 1960s and was demolished in 1965.

THORNVALE

Thornvale

William Pryor Jr. bought land at the southern edge of his family's extensive holdings in 1828, and built a modest dormered cottage, which he named Thorn Vale, probably for the dense thorn hedge that ran along the shore of the property. In 1861, Archbishop Connolly, R.C., bought the cottage as a summer retreat.

The bishop was an involved citizen, a keen advocate of Confederation and deeply committed to social justice. During the 1860s, members of all religious denominations were becoming increasingly concerned about the "moral degradation" of the lower ranks of Halifax society; the archbishop wanted help in righting these wrongs. One way he thought he could contribute was by providing a supervised refuge for some of the women he had met on his visits to Rockhead Prison. If these women had no safe place to go upon release, he reasoned, they were almost certain to return to their lives of drunkenness and prostitution.

A year after buying Thorn Vale, Connolly turned it over to Sister Clare Connolly and Sister Alexis Mooney of the Sisters of Charity, to be used as a House of Mercy. The Sisters devoted all their energy and good will to helping the former inmates, but nothing had prepared them to deal with the hardened alcoholics and delinquents brought to them. The women were supposed to be trained to sew and do laundry, as well as to receive religious instruction. They proved to be rebellious and quarrelsome, frequently fighting among themselves, or attempting to run away. The archbishop soon realized that this approach was a mistake, and after a year, the House of Mercy was closed.

The archbishop soon moved to his new residence on Dutch Village Road, selling his summer house (known by now as Thornvale) to Thomas E. Kenny in 1867. Kenny had the Pryor cottage taken down in sections and moved off the property to where it stands today on Lilac Street.

Thornvale was sold to china dealer William Webster in 1918, and stayed in his hands until he sold it to the RCMP in 1951. The house served as a residence for single men on the force, while the stables housed their mounts. With its chapel, broad porches and boathouse intact, Thornvale is one of the few remaining houses of its era.

CHAPTER 3

PARKS AND PLEASURES

Regatta on the Arm, c. 1900

TOURIST HOTELS

Armdale, when the Tupper family were in residence, before it was converted to a hotel.

The development of tourist hotels, regattas, sporting and social clubs, parks and pleasure grounds was a direct outcome of the summer homes being established on both shores of the Arm. Towards the end of the nineteenth century, several of the grand houses were converted into popular resort hotels.

In 1889 M.B. Almon Jr. placed Maplewood in the hands of the successful managers of the Queen Hotel. They had ambitious plans to turn it into a summer hotel and the house was extensively renovated. The *Morning Herald* described its new look:

> The ladies' parlour and dining room are in the northern end of the house. They can be thrown into a large room for a ballroom ... Twenty bedrooms are being furnished in walnut and gold and mahogany furniture. The walls are hung with rich engravings. On the windows are rich raw silk and lace hang-

ings. The scene from the windows is magnificent. ....The grounds are nicely laid out in serpentine walks, sheltered by maple, birch, oak, pine, fir and willow trees. There are a number of weeping acacias on the grounds which form summer houses. One in sight of the house makes a perfect tent with a clear space inside of ten feet. Under these ice cream and lunches will be served to those who visit the grounds, and luncheon and dinners will be served to parties of from ten to one hundred.

The hotel did not last, however, and in the 1890s Maplewood was once again home to M.B. Almon and available for parties, balls and long-term leases.

To the north of Maplewood, on part of the Belmont estate, plans were being drawn up for an ambitious residential community, Marlborough Woods. The development was to include a large resort hotel, The Anglo Saxon (to be designed by William Crichlow Harris), but the proponents ran into financial difficulties and the hotel was never built.

The most successful of the Arm's tourist hotels was run by F.W. Bowes, who for 10 years had been the proprietor of the Carleton House Hotel on Argyle Street. In 1906 he purchased Bloomingdale and Bircham, the Jones and Morrow houses on the Arm, and proceeded to convert Bircham. Combining the names of Bircham and Bloomingdale, the Birchdale Hotel was born. One of its first guests in 1906 was Sir Sandford Fleming, returning for a visit to Halifax and enjoying the new hotel next door to his own estate at the Lodge. Wings were added to the square mansion, first on the south and later to the north, providing elegant suites of rooms with parlours and private bathrooms, a library of 2500 volumes, a ballroom and an all-white dining room whose wall of windows looked out upon the Arm.

Birchdale was a community of its own. The comings and goings of residents along with general news of the Arm were all faithfully reported in the hotel's own newspaper, the *Birchdale Bugle*.

After Birchdale, Fred Bowes took over the former Tupper property of Armdale, intending to run it as a summer hotel. Armdale House had extensive grounds, although somewhat marred by the railway cut, and a perfect waterfront at the head of the Arm. It was built by Charles Tupper, who defeated Joseph Howe at the polls. He was a sitting member when Nova Scotia

joined Confederation, and was briefly prime minister of Canada. Bowes added a wing and brought in his son as manager, but the economic times were against them. When Bowes died, business interests blocked expansion and improvements, despite full bookings at the hotel, fearing it would interfere with establishing a modern commercial hotel in downtown Halifax. The Armdale House was converted into apartments and is now closely surrounded by city homes.

Catering to a less affluent clientele, Tom Gouley opened the three-storey Seaside Hotel in 1889 and operated a convenient outlet for alcoholic beverages. It was re-opened in 1912 by Mrs. J.T. Murphy as the Armbridge Hotel. The building was demolished in 1922.

Bircham was converted to a tourist hotel.

Armdale

ILLUMINATIONS

Preparing a float for a water carnival

Torchlight processions and decorations in the downtown, such as the one which greeted the Marquis of Lorne and Princess Louise in 1878, had become another feature of Halifax, but the Arm took the idea a step further by making the lights float and reflect upon the water. As early as 1890 when Captain Stairs was welcomed home to Fairfield, the Arm became famous for the beauty and variety of its coloured illuminations. Whenever a regatta or special occasion presented itself the residents and especially the boat clubs, lead by the North West Arm Rowing Club, would sail into action. Pleasure and racing yachts were strung with coloured lights or lanterns and decorated to form imaginative pictures. In 1905 at the celebration to mark the first Marblehead to Halifax yacht race, the favourite creation of the thousands of spectators was a floating chapel, complete with stained-glass windows, a choir whose hymns echoed over the water, and a white robed angel.

At the opening of the Memorial Tower at the Dingle in 1912 the Arm hosted an event the local paper deemed of "unparalleled importance" for which the city pulled out all the stops. The Duke of Connaught (who was Queen Victoria's youngest son) spent three days in the city, accompanied by the Duchess and their daughter Princess Patricia, which gave an intoxicating royal aura to the packed schedule of events. A delegation from Bristol, England which included the Lord Mayor, was invited to commemorate the voyage of John Cabot "the first European to tread the North American continent" as well as a host of dignitaries from Halifax and Ottawa and, of course, a proud Sir Sandford Fleming. The Canadian Club ran a poetry competition for the best poem celebrating the opening of the tower, and there was a cricket match between English-born and Canadian players.

The Governor General and his party arrived aboard the steamer *Earl Grey*, and were conveyed by tender to the special landing stage below the tower through an almost solid phalanx of small boats. The day had been declared a public holiday and both shores of the Arm, as well as the water, were packed with people. A choir of 500 schoolchildren sang the national anthem, which was followed by the dedication ceremony and the taking of official photographs. The royal party then attended a civic lunch at the Waegwoltic Club and watched the afternoon regatta.

The climax of the festivities occurred in the

Floating bandstand

evening with an illuminated boat procession and the Grand Illumination of the Arm. Preparations had been going on for weeks. A special electric cable had been laid across the Arm so that the Memorial Tower could be outlined in lights. The boat clubs prepared their displays with care — the NWARC yacht in the procession carrying a lighted scale model of the Memorial Tower. The men of HMCS *Niobe* prepared a replica of the Victory with Nelson's famous signal "England Expects..." flying from the masthead.

Scene at the Waegwaltic, North West Arm, Halifax, N.S.

On shore the Waegwoltic Club outlined its diving tower in lights and surmounted it with a canoe, stringing the club colours through the trees. Young Jim Gowan, a junior member of the NWARC remembered decorating that clubhouse with some 1500 clear glass electric bulbs which he hand-dipped in vivid dyes (coloured bulbs not yet being available) to create the effect they wanted. Every homeowner on the shores of the Arm and every owner of a boat or canoe was asked to illuminate, even if it was only with a lantern. Displays of fireworks were to be held off until 9:30 when the Grand Illumination would begin. At that time fourteen bonfires, under the supervision of selected residents on both shores, roared into life, as the homes, clubs and hotel switched on the current or

lit their lamps. The result was a display unparalleled in the city. The whole Arm was a blaze of light — forming a fitting end to a memorable day.

During the 1920s and 1930s the city of Halifax sponsored Venetian Nights on the Arm as part of Carnival Week. The western shore from the Dingle to Melville Cove was lined with red railway flares. A naval destroyer, anchored in midstream, played coloured search-lights on its own smoke or on the fleet of surrounding boats. Newspaper reports note that in 1923 Baron Byng of Vimy, the Governor General, and Lady Byng were present and boarded a launch at the Waegwoltic Club to cruise the illuminated Arm. At the Aquatic Carnival held in 1935 the Memorial Tower was floodlit, coloured searchlights played on the participants, and the Lunenburg Glee Club sang from the deck of a boat moored in the Arm. For Venetian Nights local businesses sponsored themed barges which were towed in a line up the Arm. Prizes were awarded to the best barges and to the house along the shore with the best decorations. Those who were children in the 1930s can still remember the excitement of sitting on a private dock or public wharf, legs dangling, watching the great parade which might include a fully manned pirate ship or a floating jazz band.

FLEMING'S LEGACY

View from the Dingle. Annie P. Bruce

Sir Sandford Fleming

The hillside above Thornvale remained open land until 1871 when young William Duffus began to build a unique house for his bride. Twenty-two little gabled windows dotted the sloping roofs, lighting the nine bedrooms within, and giving the house a delightful air of fantasy. Three years later, in 1874, the house, Blenheim Lodge, was sold to Sandford Fleming.

Since arriving in Halifax to begin surveys for the Intercolonial Railway, Fleming had been living on Brunswick Street. While there he came into contact with Charles Tupper, as a result of another of his interests — the effort to bring together the statesmen of the Canadas with those of the Maritime provinces. Tupper lived at the Arm, as did another of Fleming's friends, the staunch Confederation opponent Alfred Gilpin Jones. Fleming must also have known Thornvale's Archbishop Connolly, and later Thomas Kenny, both strong supporters of the Confederation project. Fleming soon turned his own attention to the Northwest Arm and its potential for recreation.

When Sandford Fleming purchased three large lots of land on the western shore in 1871, it was assumed that he was speculating. Could it be that this was intended as the Atlantic terminus of the railway, and if so would all the property in that vicinity immediately increase in value? In 1872 the *Canadian Illustrated News* could still report that "the west shore [of the Arm] remains comparatively uncultivated. It is, however, nearly all taken up by speculators for building purposes, who contemplate raising marine villas, and other improvements at no distant date." Fleming, however, was simply looking for a pleasant summer property for his family. The land he bought was already known as the Dingle; according to Fleming it had probably been named for the peninsula and bay in Ireland.

Fleming built a romantic cottage in the woods with a stone stable, and two summerhouses on high points of the property, looking down the

Below: Summerhouse Hill. Kate Lear. In the distance is Fleming's summer house at the Dingle.
Right above: Blenheim Lodge.
Right below: The gates to the Dingle.

Arm. By 1915 one had blown down in a high wind and the other caught fire. Fleming also arranged for roads to be built throughout the Dingle, including the stone banked Loop Road which still encircles Summerhouse Hill, the wooded knoll just north of the Fleming cottage.

The cottage and stable were passed on to Fleming's daughter Mrs. Thomas Critchley and her family, who used it as a summer home. Fleming's grandchildren, accompanied by a servant, rode their ponies around

the Loop Road, and in 1908 attended the laying of the cornerstone for the Memorial Tower. Fleming died at the Dingle cottage in 1915, after a brief illness.

The cottage and stable on the Dingle Road are now municipally owned properties, and the stable is used by the caretakers of the Sir Sandford Fleming Park at the Dingle. The rocky spit by the stream just north of Fairy Cove is the remains of the original wharf; in the early years of the twentieth century, children would officially inaugurate summer with a Victoria Day swim across the Arm.

Trees glistening with ice around Memorial Tower.

Both community-minded and generous, Fleming always allowed public access to the Dingle. In 1900 he wrote, "For a long time it has been a matter of great pleasure to me to see many of the citizens of Halifax innocently and healthfully enjoying themselves on my property." However, when the privilege was abused by what he called "a small knot of rowdies" who damaged the trees and played noisy games on Sundays, he reluctantly closed the Dingle to all except holders of a $1 annual permit. Concerned that he might have been depriving innocent people of their pleasure, perhaps this was the moment when he decided to eventually donate the Dingle lands to the city as a public park.

For the 150th anniversary of the Halifax meeting believed to be the first legislative assembly in the British Empire, Fleming felt that a suitable monument should be erected. He approached the city with an offer to donate the Dingle estate to the city if they would erect an ornate Italianate memorial tower. The committee appointed to discuss the tower with Sir Sandford did not see it as a municipal concern and referred him to the province. A provincial committee had already arranged for a memorial plaque to commemorate the anniversary and felt it could not involve itself in negotiations for a memorial that was expected to cost in the neighbourhood of $10,000, even if it did include a free park.

Letter-writers to newspapers had a field day. One pointed out that "the Lawson property, with extensive frontage on Williams Lake, had sold for half of what Sir Sandford expected the taxpayers of the city to expend on his tower," and another writer thought "the whole city was but a miniature park from one end to the other" and no further parkland could possibly be needed. In any case, a far more suitable location for such a monument would be on Camp Hill, far from the "disagreeable sea atmosphere" and within reach of the ordinary person. Sir Sandford, undaunted, calmly pursued the course he had decided upon. After a

On the shores of Fairy Cove c. 1900

fundraising campaign of international proportions conducted by the Halifax branch of the Canadian Club raised $23,600, the Memorial Tower, designed by the local architectural firm of Sidney Dumaresq and Andrew Cobb, was completed in 1912. The deeds to the park, which had been held in trust for the city by the Lieutenant Governor until Fleming's conditions were fulfilled, were duly handed over.

Right: Robinson's ferry at the foot of South Street

Below: Looking up the Arm. Bertha Des Clayes (1930)

CHURCHES ON THE ARM

The North West Arm Presbyterian Church (Bethany) at the head of the inlet (1890)

On the afternoon of September 27, 1896 a flotilla of little boats set out across the Arm from the Oaklands ferry dock, carrying parishioners, clergy and the full choir of St. Luke's Cathedral. The occasion was the opening of the new St. Augustine's, which had been largely paid for and furnished by the parish. It was built on land donated by Sandford Fleming after the demolition of the dilapidated mission church and school built by William Cunard in Jollimore village in 1866. So many attended that some had to stay outside the little stone building and listen to the service from under the pine tress surrounding it.

Mission churches were a popular form of outreach in mid-nineteenth century Halifax, the denominations using their buildings for both religious and educational purposes. The first was the schoolhouse built for the Anglicans at the head of the Arm in 1857 which became St. James. The Presbyterians shared the space briefly but moved to rooms in Hosterman's stone mill and, in 1867, to their own chapel on Fairmount Road.

Mrs. Harriott Lear taught a bible class for many years at the North West Arm Presbyterian Church (later Bethany Presbyterian) next to her home at Fairmount. Her eldest daughter Isabel played the organ, while younger sisters Kate and Gwendolyn taught Sunday School both for the Presbyterians and at St. Augustine's in Jollimore. Sabbath observance was important to them and on winter Sundays the sisters would often stand at the bottom of Bethany Hill, preventing skaters on their way to Chocolate Lake from using the short cut past the church.

In 1919 John Egan donated an old powder magazine at the Edmonds Grounds which had last stored munitions during the First World War, for use a Roman Catholic chapel. Despite the unusual nature of the building it became a mission church of St. Agnes. The bell came from the chapel in Holy Cross Cemetery, the little chapel that was built in a day. Later the Sisters of Charity came to teach in a parochial school attached to the new St. John the Baptist Church, built in 1929.

The first United Church service was held in Jollimore in 1951 in a former co-operative store. At the first service the seating was on planks, and the shelves were hidden from view by brown wrapping paper.

St. John the Baptist Roman Catholic Church

St. Augustine's Church, Jollimore, built in 1896.

The powder magazine that became a church.

The chapels located in the institutions on the peninsula shore of the Arm were never open to the public. The mission churches, however, that began with the schoolhouse at the Head of the Arm, have grown and still flourish today, albeit in newer buildings.

Two paintings by Kate Lear record churches of the area: (Left) William Cunard of Oaklands built an Anglican church and school in Jollimore in 1866. (Right) Bethany Church.

MELVILLE COVE

Shady Side canteen, Melville Cove

An item in an English paper as early as 1855 reported that "in the summer [Melville Island] is a great resort of the ladies of Halifax for picnics and lobster spearing. This latter amusement is carried on by torchlight — at which let no too susceptible young man attend."

In 1906 Charles Longley purchased the old Cowie and Aubony grant at Melville Cove excluding only the prison island. He subdivided and sold much of the property as cottage lots, but on the shores of Deadmans Island, the former prison burial area, he set up an amusement ground known as Melville Park. Admission was free to those who came across on Longley's ferry from the foot of Jubilee Road. A large pavilion was built and variously used as a boat house during the season, a boxing theatre and, on the upper level, a dance hall known as Kealoha. Outside were swings and slides for children. Sunday School picnic parties could go there even if it was raining to hold their races on the ground floor of the pavilion and enjoy lunches or suppers under cover. Those brave enough to venture into the basement would have seen several skulls, placed on the rafters by the proprietor when they washed out of the sandy banks or were unearthed by local residents extending their outbuildings or digging berry patches.

Canoes and boats could be hired from Joe Boutilier's at the foot of Oakland Road, Tanky Robinson's at South Street or Adam Mahar's (later Jim Mulcahy's) on Coburg Road. When the No. 9 tram line was extended down Tower Road in 1928 the transit company donated a piece of land next to the penitentiary site, where another dance pavilion was built. Below, in the little cove above Chain Rock, there were changing houses and a small beach.

Freighters moored at the head of the Arm and salvage yards were a focus for the Civic Improvement League who successfully lobbied in the 1930s to remove industrial activity and let residents enjoy the area for recreation.

Gidney's canteen and dance hall

Above and right: Children enjoyed the cool waters of the Northwest Arm during summer holidays. The barge Hellenall took children on short excursions.

DOWNS'
ZOOLOGICAL GARDENS

Andrew Downs in front of his new glass house and aviary.

During the nineteenth century amateur scientific studies and experiments were a popular pursuit. At the Northwest Arm, Robert Morrow studied fish habits at Bircham, and William Cunard conducted agricultural experiments at Oaklands. At the head of the Arm, Andrew Downs converted his interests into a memorable business — the first zoological garden in North America.

Unlike other amateur scientists at the Arm, Downs did not belong to the middle class but worked with his father and brothers in the plumbing trade. From an early age his great love was studying wildlife. He was active in the Halifax Mechanics' Institute, where he pressed for the establishment of a provincial museum of natural history and, as early as 1838, proposed a zoological park and library for the study of birds, plants and animals. When there was no response to his ideas, Downs began on his own.

In 1847 he purchased two hectares of land at the head of the Arm, and there he proceeded to establish the first zoo in North America, and to make it one of the showplaces of Halifax. His initial purchase expanded during the next 15 years to a 40-hectare park, with winding paths through the forest, past cages and pens, both open and closed, containing a wide variety of native and exotic species of birds and animals. Moose, elk and caribou had large enclosures in which to forage, with black bears and wolves inhabiting separate areas. A stream with a waterfall and artificial pond allowed a polar bear room to play, while seals, beavers and otters were supposed to be confined to fenced areas elsewhere on the stream. The seals, however, were sometimes encountered 'bumping' their way down Dutch Village Road to the Arm. Close to the house were boxes of cocoons and the bleached vertebrae of a whale which had been driven ashore some years before. Downs supplied living moose and caribou for the gardens of King Victor Emmanuel in Pisa, Italy, and California quail to the Prince of Wales, but he also claimed to have stuffed 800 moose heads; examples of his taxidermy were in museums and private collections throughout Europe and America.

Visitors said that it was possible to hear the residents of the gardens long before you could see them. The raucous cries of exotic birds were audible as far away as the public wharf at the head of the Arm where passengers alighted from excursion steamers. Proceeding up the gravelled driveway from the gate, visitors often found themselves mobbed by a variety of monkeys, birds, dogs and poultry.

The gardens were a favourite destination for family picnics and club outings at mid-century. The Caledonian Club's Scottish Gatherings were among the largest; the *Micmac* and other excursion steamers brought a thousand visitors up the Arm to the 1864 gathering.

In 1867 Downs was invited to become the superintendent of the new zoological collection in New York's Central Park. He sold his animals and birds, and the property at the Arm and moved to New York. Within three months of leaving Halifax, he was back, having decided not to accept the appointment. He managed to buy the property adjacent to his original garden, and for three years attempted to recreate his former success. It was impossible. With a few of his animals and a large collection of mounted birds, Downs retired to a house on Agricola Street and continued to correspond with the foremost naturalists of his day, and to write the occasional paper.

Walton Cottage.

Right: Monkeys were among the many creatures found at the zoological gardens

Boating, Swimming and Skating

To many Haligonians the Arm means boats — racing shells, canoes, dinghies, Roue-designed yachts or flitting sailboats in which young adults learn the ropes.

Before 1900 the waters of the Arm provided the perfect training ground for the amateur rowing crews of pilots and fishermen who were competing successfully in international races. As early as 1876 the city's bankers got together to hold an amateur double scull race on the Arm, steering clear of the increasing shipping in the harbour. Although one chairman remarked that for the first two years the participants were as much interested in the food and drink — hodgepodge and punch — as they were in the races, the Bankers' Regatta soon became an annual event. So popular were regattas at the Arm that the mayor

sometimes declared a half-holiday to allow downtown workers to attend. Military personnel who could not be spared from duty at the forts were not forgotten; their friends among the Royal Engineers sent back despatches on their crew's success by homing pigeon.

The quiet waters of the Arm also provided the perfect training ground for the amateur rowing crews of pilots and fishermen who were competing successfully in international races. The Centennial Crew, who competed in the world championships against the Thames crew of Great Britain at the American centennial celebrations in 1876, had their headquarters at Lawson's Mills. They trained three times a day on a course from Lawson's to a buoy off Horseshoe Island and back. Jerry Holland, their trainer, had made his name as a member of the Quick

Step crew of 1857, in a boat designed and built for the Continental Championships by James Pryor, whose Arm family were keen sponsors of racing activity. The Lynch brothers of Fergusons Cove, champions of Halifax County, also trained and raced on the Arm. On race days the shores would be lined with spectators, many of them wagering money on the outcome.

The growth of boating on the Arm began in 1899 when a group of people, interested in encouraging the sport of rowing, met to form a club there. Led by R.T. MacIlreith who later became mayor of Halifax, they leased a piece of land at the foot of South Street where the smooth waters of the upper Arm made a perfect racing course. The North West Arm Rowing Club (NWARC) was an instant success and in 1901 they held their first regatta. A small boathouse was built and as membership mushroomed, wings were added to the building. Soon a second storey was necessary to provide committee rooms, kitchens, an observation deck and a dance hall, for the club was intended to be both sporting and social. Women could reach this level from the boatdeck by their own staircase. On the roof was the VIP grandstand, accessible by another special stairway from the flag locker. By 1908 NWARC membership had risen to 275 with all 198 berths in the boathouse occupied. The boathouse was so crowded that R.T. MacIlreith had to loan the club a shed on his summer property across the Arm to house its racing shells until a shellhouse could be built.

In 1900 St. Mary's Aquatic Club (all of whose members belonged to the St. Mary's Christian Temperance Association and Benevolent Society) decided to move from the harbour to the quieter waters of the Arm. They briefly located next to the NWARC but soon moved on to a small yellow boathouse which they were allowed to build on Geoffrey Morrow's property Bircham, at the foot of Coburg Road. St. Mary's was strictly interested in competitive sculling and made no provision at its clubhouse for pleasure craft or social events. Their teams developed a formidable reputation both at home and abroad. Their most famous sculler was John W. O'Neill, North American Singles Champion in 1909.

On the vacated property next to the NWARC a new club sprang up in 1904 — the Halifax Amateur Boating Club (HABC). It had many influential members under President J.W. Fraser, but differed from its neighbour in not permitting alcoholic beverages on the premises. The HABC was quickly nicknamed the Halifax Anti-Booze Club while its members referred to the NWARC as "the rummy crowd" because of their practice of accepting sponsorship for regattas and out-of-town trips from liquor distributing companies. The club built what became the largest boathouse on the Arm with 275 berths and took an active part in aquatics, illuminations and concerts.

Clubs multiplied quickly in the first decade of the

The North West Arm Rowing Club (NWARC) founded in 1899

The Jubilee Boat Club, founded in 1908

Yacht racing has been popular in the Arm for more than a century

new century. In 1907 the Boulderwood Dinghy and Canoe Club was formed and held races every Saturday afternoon. A spectator remarked "to see these little sailing craft manoeuvering for the start is really a most interesting and a very pretty sight, especially as different coloured sails are beginning to make their appearance."

In 1908 the Waegwoltic Club was founded with a boathouse for 230 boats and canoes, as was the Jubilee Boat Club, which hired boats to the public. At the head of the Arm were the Independent Boating Club (later the Armdale Boat House) which brought the total number of craft using the Arm before the First World War to an estimated 1500. The sheer numbers caused the *Halifax Daily Echo* to express concern about overcrowding and safety, and it reported approvingly that plans were underway to control the boat and canoe traffic in the Arm.

Sponsoring regattas and entering trained crews in club colours became an important summer pastime for the boat clubs. The starting place was often the point at Thornvale, which divided the upper and lower basins of the Arm. The course would be rowed from Thornvale to a buoy or flag boat at Horseshoe Island and back. Later a course on the lower basin of the Arm, from South

Street to Maplewood, was sometimes used, to enable more spectators to view the events.

The historic St. Mary's Club moved for the third time to its present location on the Fairfield property in 1919 and throughout the 1920s and '30s maintained its training programmes. War canoes were an innovation when St. Mary's, the Jubilee and the North West Arm clubs first purchased them in 1920 for competition in summer regattas. Because they each required twelve paddlers and a steersman, more young people could compete in races. Russ Lownds, a young oarsman during the Depression, remembers the senior and junior crews from the club lacking the money to transport their shells to a planned regatta on the harbour. Undaunted, they rowed their eights from St. Mary's down the Arm, round the Hen and Chickens Shoal and up the harbour to compete.

With the beginning of the Second World War the club began to suffer badly. Gone were the heady days of skilled competitive crews and victorious

When the water is glassy calm, sailing can be a very leisurely event.

international scullers in the early decades of the century. The building deteriorated and the parking area became a haunt for petty criminals, prostitutes and vandals. Pollution in the Arm made the club less attractive for swimming, and boating use declined even though young women had now broken through the male-only barriers to racing the light wooden sculls.

The Sunshine Swimming Club (SSC), owned by the city, for many years provided an excellent municipal facility for sports enthusiasts at the Arm. It was managed by a swimming champion of the 1920s, Mrs. Bride Arthurs, who encouraged many

Haligonians crowded the shore to watch the boat races.

Swimming from a private dock c. 1930.

Many of the racing enthusiasts watched from boats moored in the Arm

Pearson McCurdy's house, Cottsleigh, under construction on the site of an old mill. It is now the Royal Nova Scotia Yacht Squadron's club house.

Swimmers raced from Fergusons Cove, past Purcells Cove, into the Arm to the Waegwoltic Club.

youngsters to learn to swim and to enter competitions, proudly wearing the SSC colours. The club was located between the St. Mary's and Jubilee Boat Clubs and was not luxurious — a row of cubicles with a narrow verandah along the Arm and an outhouse at the back. With a membership fee of only $2 families would often pack a picnic lunch and walk from downtown Halifax or the North End to spend the day at the Arm.

Mrs. Arthurs herself swam in a famous long distance race in 1927 sponsored by the *Halifax Herald*. The race was won by an unknown young swimmer from the St. Mary's Club, Doris Gilfoy, who completed the three-mile (almost 5 kilometres) course from Fergusons Cove to the Waegwoltic Club float in 2 hours 16 minutes. Twenty men and 18 women, including experienced racers from Massachusetts, entered the windswept and chilly waters off Fergusons Cove where the heavy seas made the swimmers' boats hard to manage. Soon the cold conditions began to take their toll as swimmer after swimmer succumbed to leg cramps and was removed from the water. By the time they entered the Arm shouts were heard from the thousands of spectators along the shore "Where are the men?" but the last man, Geddies of Sydney Mines, left the water near Boutilier's, exhausted. Twelve women finished the race, including representatives of St. Mary's, the Jubilee and the Sunshine Swimming Club.

In 1936 a group of young men who sailed small yachts on Chocolate Lake and the Arm decided to form yet another sailing club. Its first temporary headquarters was at Mosey Stoneman's Armdale boathouse, and when that was torn down the clubhouse was moved to the Edmonds Grounds. Incorporating in 1937 as the Armdale Yacht Club, membership in the early days cost only 25 cents. The club continued to grow and by the end of the Second World War consideration was being given to the now abandoned prison island in Melville Cove. Residents in the surrounding area were anxious to have the island turned over for recreational use when, at the end of the war, the island was used to store ammunition and large containers which were rumoured to contain toxic chemicals.

In 1947 the club obtained a year-to-year lease of Melville Island, at $1 a year, and by 1952 members were participating in some 250 yachting events during the season. A 99-year lease with the Department of National Defence was negotiated in 1956. Extensive renovations and additions to the former warden's house to accommodate its new role obliterated much of the original fabric of the 1808 building, the oldest

extant dwelling on the Northwest Arm. Only the steep pitch of the roof with its single dormer looking over to Deadmans Island remain as they were when J.W. Woolford sketched them in 1818-19.

When the Royal Nova Scotia Yacht Squadron (RNSYS) had to forfeit its mooring places on the harbour, the club decided to make a virtue of necessity. With the Canada Summer Games to be held in Halifax

Skating on the Arm. William Ogle Carlile (c. 1870)

in 1969 the RNSYS concentrated on training and developing its junior members who could sail their small boats in greater safety in the Arm away from the shipping lanes. Pearson McCurdy's home on the site of an old sugar refinery was purchased and money was poured into upgrading the facilities at the mill cove. A new wharf was built with water, electricity and gas hook ups, the cove was dredged to build a marina, haul-out space for the club was tripled and a marine railway was installed. The stream that had once provided power for the many industries at the cove was diverted and spanned by a small bridge to add to the attractiveness

of the grounds, while an anchor left behind in the mud of the cove bottom was cleaned up and displayed on the lawn as a reminder of the site's past.

In 1984 a small group of enthusiasts decided to bring rowing back to the Arm. The Halifax Rowing Club was incorporated using secondhand shells collected from all over Canada. The shells were kept at St. Mary's Boat Club until 1988 when the city condemned the building, leaving the club unable to get insurance. After vandals smashed the hulls of eight boats with hammers, sporting activity ceased and the city considered demolition. But the old club was firmly entrenched in the memories of generations of Haligonians — its location was unrivalled and a sympathetic city council decided to step in. In 1991 St. Mary's Boat Club reopened after $750,000 worth of renovations to its facilities, offering sculling, canoeing, community meeting space and recreational activities — this time under city auspices.

Hilda Gilkie iceboating near her home at Melville Cove (c. 1930)

Sleigh racing on the Arm

THE WAEGWOLTIC CLUB

Crowds gathered on the grounds of the Waegwoltic Club for rowing races.

The Waegwoltic, a combined social and sporting club, filled an obvious need: membership in 1908, the year it was founded, was 350 and by 1915 there were 800 active members and 1500 associates. Visits to the club that year totalled an astonishing 35,000. The club became a sort of unofficial municipal entertainment facility for important visitors to the city. Out-of-town groups like the Canadian Medical Association were granted the privileges of the club; now familiar names like R.L. Borden, C.D. Howe and Hugh McLennan were members. Royalty and vice-regal couples, including the Duke and Duchess of Connaught, the Prince of Wales, Baron and Lady Byng and Governor General Willingdon, lunched and viewed boat parades and illuminations from its verandahs.

At the beginning, members swam in the Arm and played tennis on a clay or grass court, but this was quickly improved. A large dining room with a verandah was added to the house, a boathouse built, modern swimming facilities planned, a quoits bed laid out and summer and winter entertainments provided for. The Waegwoltic Club agreed to join the NWARC and the St. Mary's Amateur Athletic Association in providing two public concerts each on their grounds during the summer season, making a delightful and popular series of events for those who listened on the lawns or from their boats on the Arm.

The Waegwoltic was one of the few private clubs that granted women equal privileges with men but certain proprieties had to be observed. For example, rules for male and female bathing costumes were spelled out in the bylaws. One daring young woman tried to improve her chances in a diving competition by removing her stockings. She was reported to the club secretary and suspended for two weeks.

A streak of social responsibility has always run through the club's affairs. There were band concerts and fund-raising events for the First World War effort, the clubhouse was turned into a hospital after the Halifax Explosion, and the Red Cross entertained returning soldiers there. Charity dances and annual fresh-air concerts were popular events. Club dance receipts sometimes went to the Sunshine Swimming Club.

Today, with a membership of more than 6,000 the Waeg goes on. Five generations of children have now learned to swim, sail and play tennis there.

This painting of Bloomingdale by Frances Jones is on display in the Waegwoltic Club, the artist's childhood home.

Tennis was played on a grass court at the Waegwoltic.

SARAGUAY CLUB

Summer Rest, Henry Lawson's summer home which became the Saraguay Club.

The purpose of the Saraguay Club, like the Waegwoltic, was primarily social. A little more exclusive than the Waegwoltic, and much smaller, its 60 original members purchased Henry Lawson's Summer Rest property in 1906 and, raising the roofline, turned the picturesque cottage with its wide verandahs into a club house. A long boathouse stood on the shore for rowboats and canoes.

In the early days access was by rowboat only. People wishing to cross the Arm went to the shore of the Pine Hill property where a horn, known as "the Hooter," rested in its box. Removing it they signalled to the ferryman at the Saraguay who would row over and pick them up.

Although it didn't have the swimming, sailing and tennis lessons offered by the Waeg, junior members still loved to go there, drinking orange crush and eating cinnamon toast while their parents played bridge on the verandah. Inside they remember the dark panelling of the entrance hall and the gloomy

pantry and kitchen where a series of beloved employees prepared lunches and dinners for members. Women and girls changed for swimming in the dilapidated boathouse but the men and boys had to make do with the surrounding shrubbery. Leading into the pine woods were the winding paths laid out by Henry Lawson, where the ground was carpeted with pink lady slippers in the spring.

By the 1950s the old house had become shabby and increasing water pollution was making children's swimming dangerous. Membership was waning and for a time the club actually closed. But devoted members rallied and built a lavish modern clubhouse overlooking the Arm to attract new members. Summer Rest was torn down and in the foundation hole the club installed a swimming pool. The improvements brought a new lease on life and today the Saraguay remains one of the city's most attractive and exclusive year-round clubs.